The Painful Truth

PALMETTO
PUBLISHING
Charleston, SC
www.PalmettoPublishing.com

Copyright © 2024 by Jhenifer N. Estevez

All rights reserved
No portion of this book may be reproduced, stored in a retrieval system, or transmitted in any form by any means—electronic, mechanical, photocopy, recording, or other—except for brief quotations in printed reviews, without prior permission of the author.

Paperback ISBN: 979-8-8229-5296-6

The Painful Truth

*Beyond Darkness:
A Journey of Acceptance
and Creation*

Jhenifer N. Estevez

With all my love

Friendships
Family
LGBTQIA family
and of course
Strangers!

This short poetry book consists of

Love
happiness, pain
my Past and Present

Dear Readers,

At first, I didn't know what to write about. I just knew that if I put my thoughts, past and present memories into words, it can become my very own poetry book. Sit back, relax and enjoy (oh! I sometimes write as if I'm talking-so pardon me!!)

      The meaning of growth, pain, family, friends, and memories is love. We search for this when we're happy, sad, in love, or lose a loved one. One day, my mother tells me, "Mija" (a Spanish word meaning daughter) the circle of life is what you experience and what you pass on as you get older. I kept asking myself why despite all the great memories I created, there is also a painful truth. Why did it hurt so much? The painful truth is who you are becoming. It is a part of your life that made you believe that it all ended, and you can't ever be the same person. Well readers, if you can check off one box, it is that there is pain in beauty and beauty in pain. Only you can define that. It is not always going to be a joyful day but in fact, a possible painful truth. That is the truth that will embrace you, challenge you and lastly, make you aware of your own experiences and story. These short-spoken words were written several years ago. Some of you reading are probably asking, "why did you just publish it?" the circle of life. We know who we are and what we desire, it doesn't necessarily mean we are always ready for the challenge. Now, I share my painful truth, with the hope that many of you can realize that the painful truth is not a place that you will stay in forever. Like myself, there's a person writing their life right now and needs a support system. Love, friendships and family are not always easy, but being accepting of your past is conceivable. There is no journey unless you get lost. Because of my painful truth, I found myself and I want to help my audience share their truth one day. You will see your own circle of life and pass it along to those who are lost, you love and cherish life with.

Maybe

TRAPPED

I want you to make love to me.
I want you to make love to my emotions.
To the scent of my perfume on my neck
To the flesh of hair on my arms.
I want you to make love to me.
But then I remembered,
You don't even love yourself.

GONE

I don't know what was more painful,
seeing you while you were gone.
Or pretending that everything was okay,
whenever you decided to come back around.
You were never here,
But thank you for wiping my tears.

OPEN BOOK

You wanted me as an open book,
and so I let you in.
You ripped every page inside of me and
made it your own story.

You befriended the closest,
Then came family;
I saw your patterns
Before I said I love you
But I didn't despise you.
I just learned to love me.
I love the woman I became.
Even when you told me that I wasn't enough.
I love the woman I left behind.
I was an open book.
That was what you told me I had to do to get to you.

Alone, once again.
This is where you left us.
Loneliness was my strength.
I guess I was just a game.
But will never be sorry.
I'm now that missing piece that you seek.
I know your puzzle is incomplete.

GREETING

I was fierce
My imperfections was my confidence.
The amount of times you knocked me down
was the only reason why I got up.
I smiled, maybe twice a day
but brighter than the first night we met.
Fierce, all over again
Just as firm as the first handshake.

SUN-UP

Pillow words became a habit.
I wanted to break them since you were never sure of me.
You insisted on late night conversations, and I didn't care.
I knew that I would wake up to a sunrise with you.
Wishing to make your favorite breakfast
just for you to leave later.

I wish every sunset was really the last one.
Every sunrise I wish you would've said love.
Why couldn't you leave at sunset and not come back?
I needed to love one sunrise before we lay on our backs.
and you lie another night.

WHAT ' IF '

I sometimes wondered what the future would be.
I wondered if it was really you.
I thought I wouldn't care if I gave you some space.
I realized the space was my parents' place.
What if I became yours?
would you have stayed?
What if I had become your space?
No, I have been betrayed.

CONSCIOUSNESS

The unknown is the best future.
Those were my words to you.
I shared them each day.
You never cared.

Conscious
but I'm lost with you.
I needed you to walk away.
I became aware.
I realized life wasn't fair.
My consciousness was enough.
There was no one to blame.

MISSED CALL

My heartbeat, after I saw your missed call.
The tremor on my fingers as I pressed call back.
Feeling the goose bumps just by seeing your name.
A missed call.
Or No caller ID instead.
That's what you wanted, all along.
To feel your presence when you were gone.

You will say hello.
You will hear the joy in my tone.
A missed call
to hear my faint breath in your ear,
oh the other side of the phone,
but a missed call
is all you ever wanted me to see.

To feel at a distant love of what could have been,
though you knew, it will never be.

SKIN

Gentle and so soft,
you described my skin.
what kind of conversations
can our skins have?
I was lost,
only craving your touch.

Nothing, but a sensitivity
skin to skin,
we wanted more than to talk.
skin to skin is what kept us 'strong.'
It was skin to skin that kept us alive.
Temporary merely not enough.

FORBIDDEN

It was the first encounter.
Our lips were sealed.
But our eyes spoke all night.
Ant then I knew,
I was your forbidden fruit and more than alright.

The thought of asking you a thousand questions,
I couldn't do it, I felt forbidden.
I made jokes to see your smile.
To show you I can make some of your hidden pain vanish after a while.
Mushing my head, while saying goodnight.
To let me know that was not goodbye.
It was your first gesture.
It was your first hello.

That hello was going to break me.
That hello made me.
How did I miss this?
You were forbidden.
And I finally accepted this.

Challenged

ALIVE

Shined from the pain that was caused.
Darkness, I tried to leave behind.
Brightness created by emptiness.
that was me,
shining from inside.
Not letting anyone into my life
Leaving enough space
for the right ones to find.

SAFE

It was the love that secured my heart.
it was the space and time.
it was the small places.
like a café with a latte.
It was the small pleasures that I chose.
My pace saved me.
It was the day I felt secure.
It was the day I knew it was over.

SURRENDER

Distant but powerful
Feeling weak but I decided to drink my tea
Felt lonely but I opened my journal
Saw your number and I inhale
I chose to dial back but I exhaled.
I knew, life would be better without you.

PROPOSAL

December fifteenth
you smiled and said that's date, to me.
I chose my happiness.
I chose my new beginning.
December you said,
My proposal,
I questioned.
You waited until I left to tell me I'm the one.
To write a poem and connect with me.
before your betrayal.
It was too late.
It was the next chapter.
It was our last day.
December fifteenth was the end.

LAUGH

I'll do anything to hear it,
those words, again
Let's not argue
Let's just laugh instead
I want your laugh
I don't want to see you cry
My laugh is all I had.
Please don't look back,
unless you want to see a frown.
Leave me with my laugh,
It is the only thing I can hold on to.

LYRICS

Listening to the songs
that made you fall apart.
The lyrics that couldn't help you
or our time apart.
Gazed softening
Heart shattering
The lyrics make sense.
Our tune no longer amazed me.

DESTINATION

We woke up the next morning.
Converse during the day.
Danced all night,
but my mind couldn't stay still all the way.

The night came.
The dreams helped me stay in bed.
You weren't my home yet,
it was easier to run away.
I prefer a vacation.
Maybe an excursion
another destination
to be fair, this felt like an addiction.

VENTURE

Loving you was just an adventure.
those were the trips that I wanted to end.
I always got ready,
to see you disappear.
My heart was getting ready.
to solemnly shed in tears

I COULDN'T WAIT

Blaming myself
this was the choice I made.
What did you see in me?
If it wasn't easy

Love me now
not my past
How much longer?
I always asked.

It's better now,
if I let you go.
It's better now,
as the answers are a blur.

NEXT TIME

To tore to trust again.
Turning off the cell in its place,
that didn't erase the memories or the face.
Nurturing myself
And I revived from my pain.
If I could choose to do this again,
I choose my heart to trust you in different ways.

Healing

TENDER

She thought you were different.
This is what you told her.
Her actions were consistent.
but for a short while.
She was tender like her soft smile.
And it was easy to forget about the pain she recently caused her.
She thought her search for love was over.
but the truth was she already knew you were tired of her.

LOVE ME AT NIGHT

Loving her was easy.
She let her in.
During the sunrise she felt empty
and one night she felt complete.

Broken into pieces.
as she didn't know what that day will bring
loving her with the moon
but she felt alone with the sunlight.

Love me at night or leave at peace.
Will you come back for me?
The truth was she wanted you to kiss her bottom lip.
she was sure it was the last goodbye,
Even that was a lie.

Jhenifer N. Estevez

FOUND

Was I wrong to ask you to wait?
To stay and watch me plant my seed.
It will all go away,
Those are the only words that made sense to me.
Thinking that she gave up.
But she didn't meet me halfway.
Easy enough to say.
I want to be found.
Grow together and stay in our place.

EVENTS

Love had her confused,
she smiles from all the events.
Although the events were long gone,
and all she can do was wait for the next day
to have a drink in her hand.

The smell of the alcohol on her breath
I smirked instead.
I could heal from the words she's been spilling.
Wondering if by that time
she even knew what day of the week it was.

THIRD TIME

Waiting for a different outcome.
That is what she hoped for.
The third time was a charm.
It was the number you rely on.
You were misleading or just an act?
Third time and not our last.

SEARCHING

Empty,
Just searching for who I think I may be.
Not easy, feels like it is storming.
How can I smile?
Why am I not finding what's supposed to be found?

Beyond, I've looked.
Promises weren't kept.
Just one thing to do, I will accept.
Not hard to let go.
These are the steps I'm taking to become my best,
in a place I want to be fearless.

Not all things need to be seen,
my actions will speak.
I rather feel.

A simple individual
That is what you told me.
I wasn't searching for a beast.
Your weakness was seen as a mystery.
Where will I be?
In fact,
I hope you'll never find me.

GULLIBLE

Never thought once again
Another tear ran down this face.
To a feeling without definition.
To a feeling with one simple meaning.
A heart that is not mine,
with an open mind so close by.
Not walking out
Not giving in
are you being gullible or discrete?

The actions unspoken.
The silence being read.
What to expect, knowing that I'm not in her head.
Giving this heart another chance
one day, you'll be full again.
Don't worry.
There was nothing left unexplained.
Never thought once again,
one kiss will make feel gullible.
one kiss will make feel this way.

BLINDSIDED

To wake up and do the same morning routine,
and pretend to just be.
To unfold yesterday's pain and make it a better day.
To love me for what I did instead of what could have been.
Enjoy the present moment, they said
but how much weight can this life take from me?
Patiently waiting for the pleasure, I seek for
I was blindsided by your own perception.

CHISELED

She doesn't wear make up
It makes her feel alive
Admiring the small brown freckles on the side.
Why cover any part of it?
It doesn't make her feel any less
It makes her glow.
Letting the pain fade away.

BOND

Walking by the age of two
Walking with the limp that you noticed
My favorite memory of us two
It was the year 1992

You spoiled me
You never said no to me
I was held with the same love you now hate me with
Even if this is not real
This is how you made me feel.
It was the best bond.
I'm glad you didn't say no to the surgery.
You need to know that you saved me.
Now that you know the real me,
I'm okay with us not speaking.

I'm Home

DROWNING

When you didn't see your worth
I saw your strength.
When you didn't recognize your why
You were shown purpose.
When you couldn't breath
I was willing to take your last breath.
I was drowning for you.
yet, you never saw me.
That didn't break me.
I was drowning for your love,
I saved my heart instead.

SILENCE

Listening to my thoughts
Viewing your body
Feeling my feelings
While your chest rises with each breath you take.

In silence
That's when I feel you most.
In silence I crave your voice
What you're keeping in are those pieces of you I desire to devour.
In silence you never judge.
You understood me the most.
In Silence, you pushed me away.
and I never spoke to you again.

CONSISTENT

Admitting to the fear
Releasing the mixed feelings
Then thinking to yourself, when would I be at ease?
That smile, it is my consistency.
That is my key.
My lead, not knowing where I would be.
My positivism to all the needs.
Even if I take a wrong step, it is me.
It is my consistency.

THE SHEET

I had a navy-blue sheet.
The color sheet I felt deeper in love on
As I lay down beside you
What way should my body lean?
It never mattered.
As long it is you I'm blending with.

A navy-blue sheet,
that didn't quite fit.
I shall change you.
one day I won't remember the memories on you.

Not the color sheet I lay on
The new sheet I want to resemble.
A navy-blue sheet
it is just another part of me.

When I change you tomorrow
Then, whom would I be?
Maybe, my next sheet?
This was the last piece of blue sheet you'll share with me.

WITHOUT YOU

I stopped wondering.
I stopped assuming.
I started understanding.
not everyone can be empathetic.
I stopped trying to pretend that everything is okay.
I started accepting that this is pain.
I know that pain is not a weakness.
I know that pain became my strength.
I love that I'm not alone.
but I dislike how long is taking me to show that without you.
I know who I am.
I'm not waiting for another day.
I'm better today.

FIREFLIES

I miss the number of kisses you wanted in a minute.
I felt like I was in a field with fireflies.
I thought you were just needy.
I thought you were just annoying.
I laughed,
I knew I was falling for you.
But I was only hiding.
The number of kisses you wanted in a minute.
Do you remember when I told you?
You're not a firefly moment.
And you will not be my maybe.

ENDLESSLY

When I think of you
I think of me
When I think of me
I think of us
When I think of us
a light of eternity rises above.
This constant smile
I do know how to love.
You are my forever moment.
The one I didn't have to search for.

WISHES

I remembered sitting on the grass with a glass of wine.
Moscato, our favorite.
I remembered wishing for love as I took a sip.
I remembered that wish.
because I closed my eyes, and we've kissed.

DISBELIEF

I felt sorrow
I felt misery
At times I didn't know how to feel.

Insensitive to the world
This is not me.
You never showed me authenticity
You were right about one thing.

You were never my person
and that I believed.
Only time will tell
it was finally easy to be me.
It was easy to breathe.

LOVE

You never cherished my presence.
That is why my thoughts were unspoken.
You didn't feel alive.
I just knew you were a lie.
I thank you for my past.

I was always woman enough.
Now, all I need is the essence of my existence.
I chose me
I chose Love.
I am free.

The Painful Truth

"Trust your intuition and be guided by love."
- *Charles Einstein*

"I am not what happened to me. I am what I choose to become."
- *Carl Jung*

Thank you!

The Painful Truth

'I feel lost, and I don't know what to do or say anymore', are common words we say and face day to day. Despite what happened yesterday or years ago, we truly have one life to live, we have today. Loving and accepting things that you can't change will empower you.

Poetry brings peace, joy and a sense of clarity to life. Feelings and emotions transition every second of the day and if these words resonate with you, this poetry book can redirect and even help you make better choices. All relationships are fundamental. Love is beautiful, take your time on your journey because you truly are an inspiration to someone else.

www.ingramcontent.com/pod-product-compliance
Ingram Content Group UK Ltd.
Pitfield, Milton Keynes, MK11 3LW, UK
UKHW022211230426
12048UKWH00016BA/777